Table of Contents

Page

DISCLAIMER i

LIST OF ILLUSTRATIONS ii

LIST OF TABLES iii

PREFACE iv

INTRODUCTION AND BACKGROUND 1

FUTENMA REPLACEMENT FACILITY 6

UNITED STATES-JAPAN ROAMAP FOR REALIGNMENT 7

US-JAPAN AGREEMENT TO RELOCATE III MEF TO GUAM 8

PRESIDENT OBAMA-PRIME MINISTER HATAJOMA PRESS CONFERENCE 9

JAPANESE POLITICAL SITUATION 11

AGREED IMPLEMENTATION PLAN (AIP) FORCE LAYDOWN 12

    AIP Headquarters Elements Shift 14
    Command and Control Concerns 16
    Tyranny of Distance 16
    Logistics Challenges 18
    Training 20

PROPOSED COURSE OF ACTION 25

CONCLUSION 26

NOTES 27

BIBLIOGRAPHY 29

Illustrations

Page

Figure 1. Okinawa Consolidation 4

Figure 2. AIP-directed Laydown.. 13

Figure 3. Tyranny Distance.. 17

Figure 4. Marine Times Map of Guam & Tinian... 24

Tables

Page

Table 1. Guam Strategic Lift for Training Cost Summary 19

Preface

The Department of Defense, in particular the United States Marine Corps, is facing

potentially drastic changes to its force posture that will ultimately shift a major portion of the

nation's 911 force in readiness away from America's threats in the Pacific. I chose this topic due

to my assignment as an Action Officer (AO) to the newly established Plans, Policies and

Operations, Pacific Division (PP&O/PD). During my brief six-month stay at PPO/PD, I noticed

that some major difficulties were being addressed and overcame on a daily basis by hardworking

and dedicated Staff Officers in Headquarters, Marine Corps as a result of an International

Agreement (IA) that did not take into consideration Marine Corps training requirements,

command and control needs, and other aviation and base realignment concerns.

I would like to thank Dr. Bruce E. Bechtol Jr., Professor of International Relations at Marine

Corps University for his guidance and mentorship during my research and preparation of this

research paper. I would also like to extend my gratitude to Major Michael Cho, Action Officer,

Headquarters, Marine Corps, PPO/PD for his assistance and guidance provided to me while I

attempted to put my arms around this complicated and controversial issue. I want to thank him

for his many months of hard and thankless work while we were colleagues at PPO/PD and his

patience as he broke me in as a newly assigned Action Officer. I would like to send my thanks

to Mr. Bruce Klingner, Senior Research Fellow for Northeast Asia in the Asian Studies Center at

The Heritage Foundation for his candor and willingness to educate a novice like myself

regarding the complex issues surrounding foreign affairs issues in the Pacific region. Lastly, I

would like to thank the staff of the Gray Research Center and the Marine Corps University

Library for their professionalism, expertise, and patience during my research.

"[The agreed road map] "may not be the perfect alternative for anyone, but it is the best alternative for everyone. And it is time to move on,"

- Robert Gates, Secretary of Defense

"So, they all made a 106 mile round trip in the God forsaken desert under furnace- like conditions to eat unpalatable food in a dingy cafeteria, a trip nobody had been looking forward to and nobody wanted to take."

- The "Road to Abilene" story by Jerry Harvey as told by the Reverend John H. Nichols

The decision to realign USMC forces from Okinawa to Guam is an ill-conceived vision driven by Japanese politics, a weak U.S. counter-response, coupled with poor planning has ill-postured USMC forces to confront the existing and emerging threats in the Pacific region. For more than thirteen years the Department of Defense (DoD) has conducted reviews, studies, analysis, and debates regarding what the appropriate United States defense posture stance should look like in the Pacific Command (PACOM) Area of Operations (AO). Beginning in 1996 with the joint U.S.-Japan governmental committee regarding the return of Marine Corps Air Station Futenma to Japan, both countries have been interlocked in international negotiations, complex force logistical requirement calculations and operational planning along with budgetary debates between the respective countries and within each nation's governmental agencies. The decision to realign forces within the Pacific region will have lasting national defense implications for both governments and will essentially establish the United States force posture stance for the next fifty or more years. Each respective nations' leadership must understand the gravity and realities associated with such an endeavor currently being undertaken and put aside all political agendas or frivolous debates in order to ensure this decision is not taken lightly and presents the appropriate posture required to address the current and future threats within the PACOM Area of Operations. At the heart of the Pacific realignment is the relocation of 8,000 United States Marine Corps (USMC) forces from Okinawa to the unincorporated organized Territory of Guam and the relocation of Marine Corps Air Station Futenma. Current international agreements between both countries have the Marine Corps relocating forces and dependents to Guam by 2014 in order to reduce the impact of daily operations by the United States military presence on Okinawa and the associated impact on the civilian populace. The above quote taken from Secretary of Defense Robert F. Gates during his visit to Japan in October 2009 with senior Japanese administration officials should be taken very seriously and one should ask if this truly is the perfect alternative.[1] The current realignment as proposed by both governments is a poorly conceived vision coupled with inadequate and complex planning agencies all vying for their respective interests. Should we move on with a plan to alter America's force posture in the Pacific simply for the sake of appeasement and inability to stand firm during international negotiations that would positively reinforce our own national security interests?

Several issues are currently being studied and possibly renegotiated between the two countries and within their respective cabinets, defense agencies and other government entities. The binding documents established in 2006 between Japan and the United States list nineteen Agreed Implementation Plans (AIP) that describe and facilitate the internal base consolidations, U.S. military force relocations within Okinawa and Japan, the relocation of identified units from Okinawa to Guam, budget responsibilities and other key agreements critical to the effective transfer of property and shifting of USMC personnel in the PACOM Area of Operations.

There currently exist five major tenants to the international agreement that directly affects USMC forces on Okinawa. The Futenma Replacement Facility (FRF) and its relocation from

Marine Corps Air Station Futenma to the soon-to-be constructed air facility developed at Camp Schwab is to date the most controversial issue on both sides of the two governments. The essential lynchpin for the entire realignment of forces as stated in the Roadmap for Realignment and which the position is continuously reinforced by the Marine Corps, is that tangible progress toward the completion of the FRF at Camp Schwab is a prerequisite for other Marine Corps realignments. The second major issue is the Guam Master Plan that details responsibilities for cost sharing and bi-lateral training opportunities on United States soil. The cost of the approximate relocation of 8,000 Marines and dependents from various headquarters elements of III Marine Expeditionary Force to Guam will be paid in part by Japan at a cost of 6.09B and the U.S. commitment being 4.18B as prescribed in the Roadmap. Third, specific headquarters units will relocate to Guam once adequate facilities are completed. Fourthly, the Marine Corps Air Station Iwakuni Master Plan which prescribes the relocation of Carrier Air Wing Five (CVW-5) fixed wing squadrons from Naval Air Facility Atsugi to MCAS Iwakuni, the Marine Air Refueling Squadron VMA-152 will be shifted from MCAS Futenma to MCAS Iwakuni along with appropriately shifted airspace to accommodate the reallocation of aircraft. Lastly, the controversial issue of Okinawa consolidation of bases south of Camp Foster, and identified areas aboard Camp Foster to be returned to the Japanese, and in particular, the Okinawa community with USMC forces consolidating on remaining bases aboard Okinawa with the preponderance aboard Camp Schwab. This action will potentially reduce the urban impact to the local communities partially affected by the American presence while shifting American forces to the less congested areas surrounding Camp Schwab. Figure 1[2]

American military planners have worked diligently within the various departments of the Office of the Secretary of Defense, Department of the Navy, Headquarters Marine Corps, the

Joint Guam Program Office, and other lower-level governmental agencies within the United States and Japanese governments to effectively institute the plans laid forth by the key negotiators within the U.S. Department of State (DOS) and the Japanese Ministry of Foreign

Okinawa Consolidation

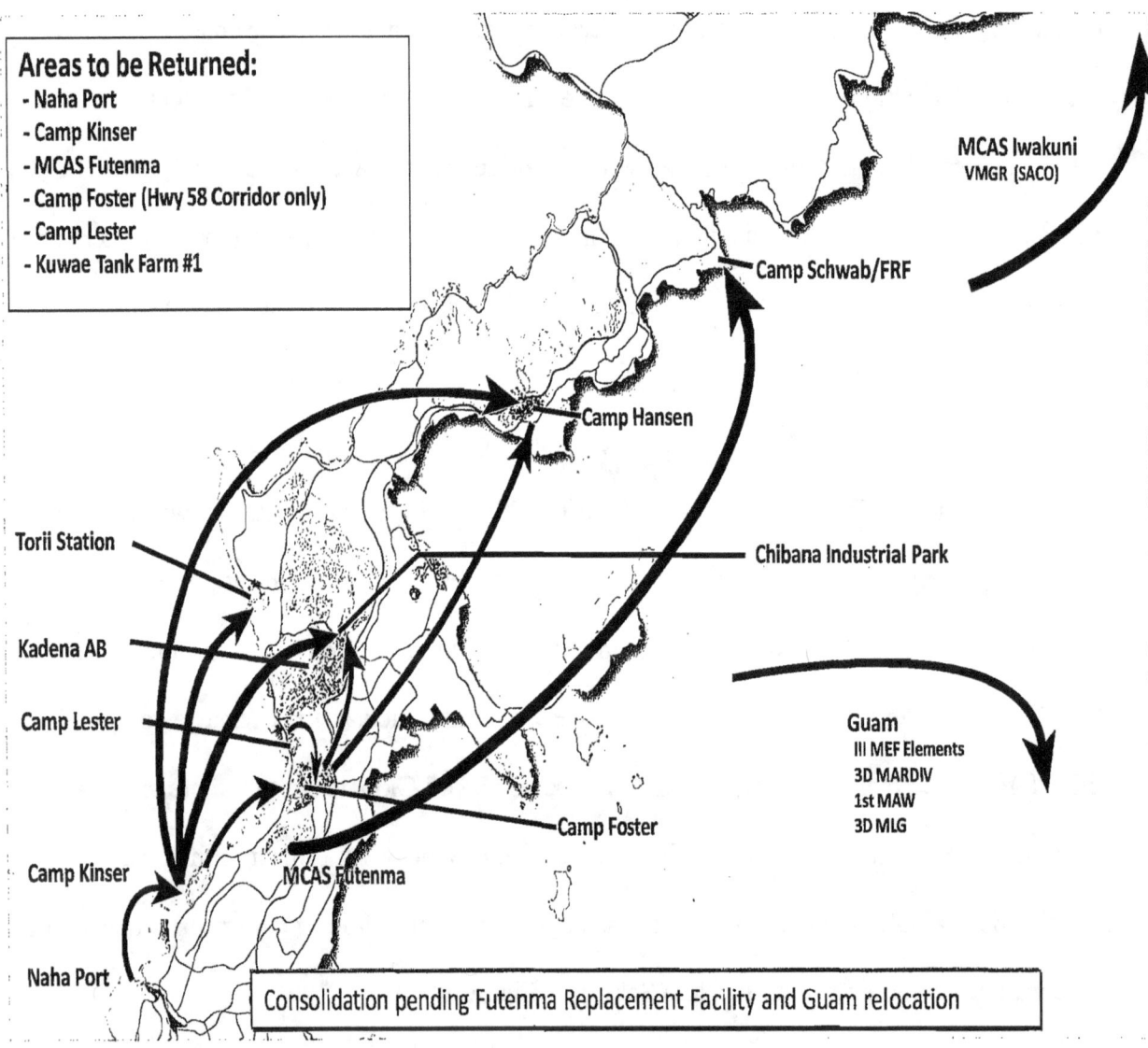

Areas to be Returned:
- Naha Port
- Camp Kinser
- MCAS Futenma
- Camp Foster (Hwy 58 Corridor only)
- Camp Lester
- Kuwae Tank Farm #1

MCAS Iwakuni
VMGR (SACO)

Camp Schwab/FRF

Camp Hansen

Torii Station

Chibana Industrial Park

Kadena AB

Camp Lester

Guam
III MEF Elements
3D MARDIV
1st MAW
3D MLG

Camp Foster

Camp Kinser

MCAS Futenma

Naha Port

Consolidation pending Futenma Replacement Facility and Guam relocation

Figure 1   Source: HQMC/PP&O/Pacific Division 2009

Affairs (MOFA). Key issues listed above involving the FRF, base consolidations across Okinawa, environmental impact concerns on both Okinawa and Guam, training capabilities across the Marianas and infrastructure concerns associated with such a massive relocation of Marine Corps forces, dependents and unit equipment have either been partially addressed, fairy-dusted or the assumption has been made that no further discussions are required based on all parties being in complete agreement of the respective details listed in the nineteen AIPs established in the bi-lateral negotiations and subsequent international agreements. One would hope that the strategy of working out the rest of the details of the International Agreement, as long as both nations can agree to something, was not considered. Yet, based on the continuous FRF controversy, the lack of detailed thought on force laydown and associated training needs to match the laydown, one would have to believe that expediency in ensuring the perception that progress had been made in solving the concern of the Japanese constituents was accomplished at the expense of U.S. national interests.

In any matters of international importance, either political or military involving issues such as the relocation of more than 8,000 Marines and Sailors plus their dependents and other government civilian employees, one should have a basic grasp of the events that led up to the decision to permanently alter the defense force posture of the U.S. in the Pacific. The 1951 security treaty following World War II created the initial setting for U.S. forces on Japan which was subsequently followed by the 1960 Treaty of Mutual Cooperation and Security which allowed for U.S. military facilities to be stationed on Japanese soil and served as a stabilizer for security within the Pacific serving the national security interests of both countries and ultimately benefiting all U.S. allies in the region. On December 2, 1996, the Special Action Committee on Okinawa (SACO), established by the Governments of Japan and the United States released their

5

final report regarding both countries initiatives to reduce the burden on the people of Okinawa and thereby strengthening the Japanese-U.S. alliance.[3] The goals for this committee were clear: conduct a twelve-month review to provide to the Security Consultative Committee (SCC) on ways to realign, consolidate and reduce U.S. facilities and areas, and adjust operational procedures of U.S. forces in Okinawa consistent with their respective obligations under the Treaty of Mutual Cooperation and Security and other agreements.[4] This report would ultimately lay the groundwork for future negotiations and ultimately be the catalyst for today's nineteen classified Agreed Implementation Plans currently being "reviewed" to ensure those plans can be properly executed.

A couple of issues regarding this report surfaced that directly affects United States Marine Corps forces within III MEF. Firstly, the return of Futenma Air Station to Okinawa, Japan within the next five to seven years after adequate facilities are completed and operational was the most notable. Given the report's timeline, the Futenma facility would have been in Japan's control by 2003. This deadline came and went without the deadline coming to fruition. This pattern will continue to the present and will undoubtedly continue past the year 2020 and beyond based on unrealistic and costly timelines. The second issue is the required recommendation to the SCC for a candidate Sea-based Facility (SBF) area to the SCC as soon as possible and formulate a detailed implementation plan no later than December 1997.[5] Along with other minor issues addressed by the Government of Japan, this document is considered to be the seed that formulated a way-ahead for the future relocation, in particular the plan for the Futenma Replacement Facility. The sea-based facility will essentially be the FRF located at Camp Schwab constructed in waters adjacent to Camp Schwab built on reclaimed soil from the bottom of the Henoko waters, a key habitat for the Dugong which has presented legal obstacles from both Japanese activists and, most incredibly, from courts from within the United States. [6] In 1999, the Governor of Okinawa announced the planned relocation of the FRF to Camp Schwab on the east coast of the island. In November 1999, Governor of Okinawa Prefecture Keiichi Inamine announced the coastal area around Henoko, Nago City, within the Camp Schwab Water area, as a candidate site for relocation, to which Mayor Tateo Kishimoto of Nago City approved in December of that same year. [7] In 2002, both governments established the Defense Policy Review Initiative (DPRI) for review of the nation's strategic objectives, defense cooperation and U.S. basing issues. In 2005, the United States offered the relocation of USMC forces from Okinawa to Guam to assist in the basing effort and reduce the impact of military operations on the daily lives of the Okinawa people.

What can be described as the most important document surrounding the entire relocation and consolidation of USMC forces from Okinawa to Guam is the May 1st, 2006 United States-Japan Roadmap for Realignment Implementation. [8] U.S. Secretary of State Condoleezza Rice with the Secretary of Defense Donald Rumsfeld agreed to terms with the international agreement with the government of Japan represented by Minister of Foreign Affairs Taro Aso and Minister of State for Defense Fukushiro Nukaga. [9] This so-called "Roadmap" is a summary of the nineteen Agreed Implementation Plans that are classified Confidential and is associated with the United States force relocations and consolidations on Okinawa, Japan, and Guam. The Roadmap is an unclassified description of the way-ahead and forms the basis for the general awareness for the international community of the Japanese-United States agreement based on the two "equal partners" within the bi-nation alliance.

The Roadmap signed by both countries is legally binding and has presented plenty of controversy between the U.S. and Japan and within each respective nation regarding the specifics detailed in six major areas of the agreement. The Roadmap is filled with vague terms of conditions, the unrealistic deadline of 2014, the major shift in USMC forces without the clear understanding to the ramifications to the people of Guam and the simplistic look at funding responsibilities associated with each respective government. Nonetheless, the document clearly states what is required of both governments to reduce the military impact of the island of Okinawa. Every major issue, negotiation and controversy ultimately refers back to the May 1st, 2006 agreement with clearly identifies the significance and complexity of this document.

One additional agreement signed on February 17th, 2009 by the current United States Secretary of State, Hillary Rodham Clinton and the current Minister of Foreign Affairs Yukio Hatoyama further cemented the May 1st, 2006 agreement by, "Recalling that, at the meeting of the United States-Japan Security Consultative Committee on May 1st, 2006, the Ministers recognized that the implementation of the realignment initiatives...will lead to a new phase in alliance cooperation, and reduce the burden on local communities, including those on Okinawa, thereby providing the basis for enhanced public support for the security alliance,"[10] Based on this new agreement, there can be no doubt that the relocation and consolidation is moving forward and the U.S. military planners will be faced with a monumental challenge of planning for the largest realignment of U.S. forces since the end of World War II. Currently Plans, Policies and Operations, Headquarters Marine Corps is working on the guidance as provided via the United States Roadmap for Realignment Implementation plan set forth in 2006 between Japan and the United States. HQMC Action Officers working with the current Roadmap established at the political level that does not represent basic USMC operational doctrine and is out of touch with logistical timelines has caused an increase in workload and planning to prepare for the ultimate scenario of dismantling the essential details of the current agreement with orders to execute "Plan B"; a plan which is currently not authorized to be on the public table of discussion.

One should also have an understanding of the political aspect of the Marine relocation to Guam. As Bruce Klingner, the Senior Research Fellow for Northeast Asia in the Asian Studies Center at the Heritage Foundation, states in his December 15, 2009 Backgrounder article, "Attempts by the new Japanese government to renegotiate terms of the Guam Agreement, which would realign U.S. military forces in Japan, have seriously strained U.S.-Japan relations, harming the bilateral military alliance.[11]

On November 13, 2009, U.S. President Barack Obama and Prime Minister Yukio Hatayoma of Japan held a Joint Press Conference during President Obama's first official Presidential trip to Japan reiterating the United States and Japan as equal partners in the U.S.-Japan alliance and that will be reflected in the resolution of the base realignment issues related to Futenma.[12] The President further pressed upon the issue that the goal remains the same by providing for the defense of Japan with minimal intrusion on the lives of the people who share the space with our military. President Obama during the same joint conference also stated that, "Each country brings specific assets and strengths to the relationship, but we proceed based on mutual interests and mutual respect, and that will continue." Does an equal partnership really exist between the two countries in respect to bilateral security partnerships or commitment to previous international agreements or does one exist merely by perception alone without any real substance provided by the Government of Japan and with heavy participation of the Government of the United States? As Michael Auslin writes in the January 2010 Outlook Series addition for the American Enterprise Institute, "Japan takes the lead as the centerpiece for democracy in the region with the United States continuing to be the foundation for the global and regional security for the foreseeable future."[13] He further states in the article that the costs and difficulties of maintaining the alliance are far outweighed by the benefits the alliance continues to bring to Japan, the United States, and Asia as a whole. The perception exists that both present equal status in the alliance, but why would the Japanese government continue to jeopardize the relations with the United States, which overwhelming contributes to the safety and security of the Japanese people from the continuing and emerging threats within the region. Transferring critical USMC forces off the island of Okinawa only degrades the security cooperation between both countries while presenting little benefit other than noise and population reduction on Okinawa while further splitting American forces from the epicenter of the American-Japanese alliance. Bruce Klingner, in his Web Memo posted for The Heritage Foundation on August 31, 2009, states that, "But it is clear that the DPJ will be less willing to fulfill existing bilateral U.S. force realignment agreements and more resistant to Washington's requests for Japan to expand its overseas security role."[14] Japan's two-front resistance to step up their efforts in the Global War on Terror and their commitment to formalized agreements with the U.S. because it doesn't serve their national interests is selfish and ultimately a dangerous course of action.

In addition, the political flavor within Japan is one of disagreement with the U.S. in regards to overseas commitments in Afghanistan, refueling operations in the Indian Ocean, and one of altering Japan's self-defense guidelines to allow for a more robust overseas defense role.[15] The simple answer is that a co-equal partnership is severely lacking between both countries and Japan has demonstrated its lack of maturation as a participating member in the international community of armed forces capable, or willing, of submitting what is necessary to the bilateral relationship beyond what serves their own national interests.

During the 2009 Japanese lower house legislative election, the soon-to-be elected liberal Democratic Party of Japan (DPJ) ran on a campaign promise to revise the previously agreed upon international force realignment agreement.[16] This cause appealed to many citizens of Japan, in particular Okinawans, because no one wants the FRF to reside in their backyards with the perception of shifting the "problem" of the FRF from one community to another or the acquiescence of further U.S. troops on Japanese soil. The United States has been vigorously maintaining that this agreement must be adhered to by both countries since this agreement lies at the heart of the entire DPRI in the Pacific concept that ensures USMC forces are not improperly degraded in their ability to maintain capabilities in the PACOM AOR. Bruce Klingner states the DPJ won their 2009 election with emphasis placed on domestic issues, a strategy that will continue during domination of the Diet, and that Japan appears complacent, willing to cede the Asian leadership role to China.[17] For the first time in 50 years, a liberal Japanese party has had control in the Diet, a party that shows remarkable similarities to the current American administration. A similarity that one would expect in regards to mutual cooperation, understanding, and a propensity for action based on like ideologies. Yet, during the past year anything but forward political action has been produced. On January 6, 2010 Press Secretary Geoff Morrell explained that the U.S. does not accept the May deadline by the Japanese Government requesting to further discuss internally on the relocation of the FRF and called on Tokyo to promptly resolve the issue.[18] Internal turmoil within the DPJ has also fueled the uncertainty regarding Japan's commitment to the International Agreement with the head of the Social Democratic Party threatening to pull out of the DPJ party coalition if the FRF stays on Okinawa.[19]

With Japan's reluctance to pursue the obligations set forth in the 2006 agreement, the United States should step back from the ill-advised agreement and extend the offer to restart the renegotiations from scratch and create a plan that makes sense for both countries. A plan that does not shift U.S. forces farther from the strategic center of gravity within PACOM and one that continues to properly provide for the security of our Japanese ally as set forth in the 1960 Security Cooperation Treaty signed by both countries is not just a good idea, but required in order to ensure the regional threats that reside in the PACOM Area of Operations receive a strong message that the United States is not pulling away, but strengthening their position to respond. Given the complexity of the proposed relocation of Marines and Sailors to Guam, a possible solution to ensure both countries are pursuing the right strategic and establishing sound policy would be to have both governments with newly elected leaders direct a complete review of the previously signed international agreements, evaluate our current threats in the regions in regards to terrorism and conventional military force threats, and determine a way-ahead that is inclusive and addresses the needs of both governments.

The AIP-directed force laydown directly or indirectly involves approximately 27,300 Marines, Sailors, base employees and dependents. Based on the details resident within the Roadmap, the population of USMC forces affected is based on Pre-OIF calculations.[20] The shift of 8,000 Marines and Sailors from the island of Okinawa to the unincorporated Territory of Guam will be executed to assist in reducing the impact of military operations on the local Okinawa populace. In essence, the plan prescribes for the headquarters elements and associated personnel to relocate to Guam while the main body, the meat of III Marine Expeditionary Force's air and ground team, to remain on Okinawa. This relocation will result in 8,000 Marines, Sailors and approximately 9,000 civilian dependents to now operate on the territory of

Guam vice Okinawa. This will present a dramatic increase in population and cultural impact on the people of Guam while relieving the current impact of daily military operations on the Okinawans. According to a November 13, 2009 Government Accountability Report regarding Guam Infrastructure Impacts relating to the military build-up, the current military population will increase from 15,000 in 2009 to about 29,000 in 2014 causing a 15% increase in overall population from 178,4300 to more than 205,195.[21] The breakdown of force personnel as listed in Figure 2 presents immediate questions once an individual has an opportunity to review the force laydown. The same GAO report lists major improvements to the existing infrastructure based on the inadequacy of being able to support the 15% increase in population.

AIP-directed laydown

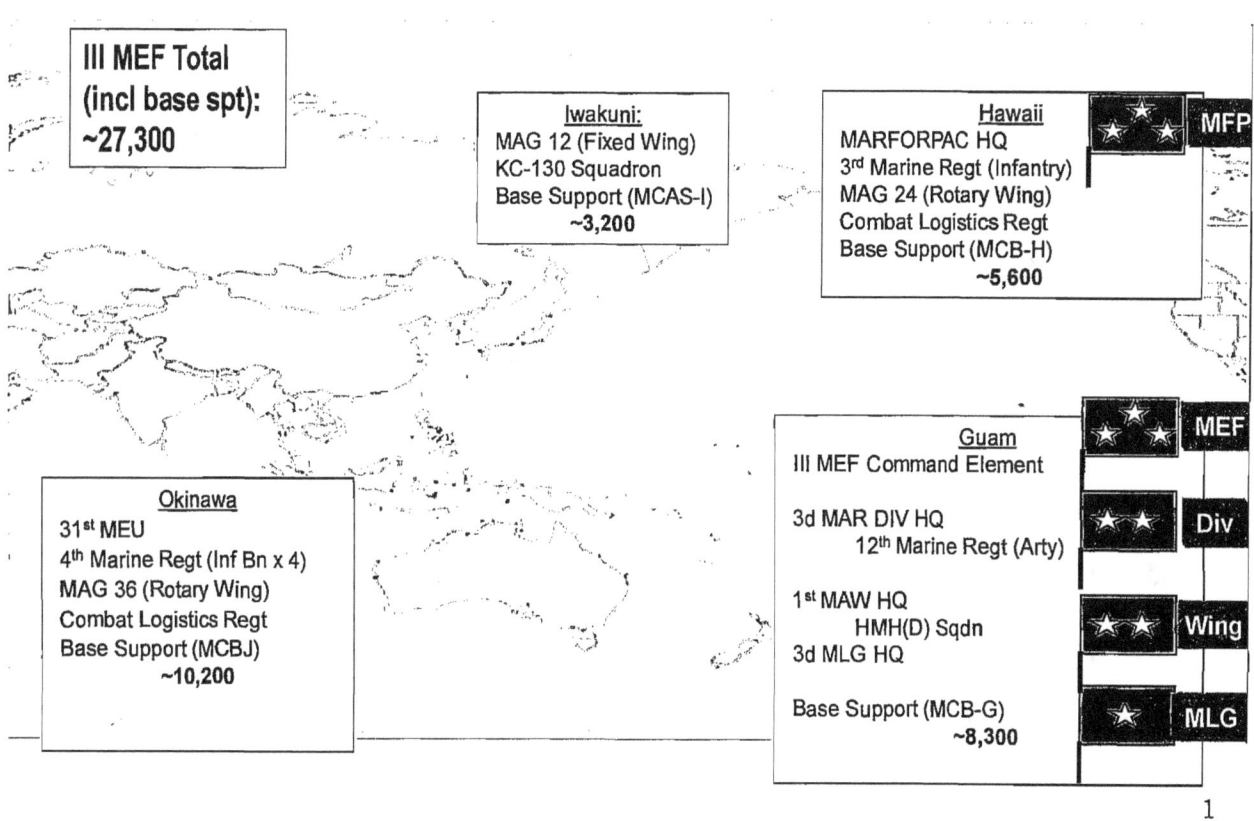

Figure 2   Source: HQMC/PP&O/Pacific Division 2009

Major improvements include road infrastructure, electric power production, waste management services, potable water production and other essential services. Any city or region acquiring a 15% percent population increase would experience major infrastructure challenges and add the logistical challenge of being in the middle of the Pacific Ocean where costs for basic goods and services are already expensive. This move simply does not financially set the U.S. Government up for success and remains one of the many anchors dragging the argument for altering our defense posture.

A major concern of the force laydown that is easily identifiable is that the headquarters elements of the major force elements of III MEF are all relocating to the island of Guam. III MEF's Command Element (CE), 3rd Marine Division's Headquarters along with the headquarters element of the 12th Marine Regiment, 1st Marine Air Wing Headquarters, and the 3rd Marine Logistics Group Headquarters will be relocating in its entirety. In total, approximately 8,300 Marines and Sailors will make the transition and commence operations and training aboard Guam while still managing the day-to-day operations of their respective forces on Okinawa. Along with the shift to Guam, although not part of any U.S.-Japan agreements, Hawaii's total force strength will improve to 5,600 Marines and Sailors of the Marine Forces Pacific Headquarters, 3rd Marine Regiment Headquarters, the headquarters element of Marine Air Group 24 and an unidentified Combat Logistics Regiment. With this shift from Okinawa, Iwakuni will see a total of 3,200 within fixed wing MAG Headquarters and a KC-130 squadron with associated base support personnel. What will remain on Okinawa will be approximately 10, 200 Marines, Sailors and base support personnel, not including the numbers of dependents still authorized residence on Okinawa.

One would have to assume that if you remove the snake from the body, there would be at least some semblance of a headquarters unit to mind the main body. With more than 10,000 American troops and double the numbers for dependents and base support personnel, the reduced impact on Okinawa is marginal, at best, given the other services stationed on Okinawa. Approximately 17,000 Americans departing the island of Okinawa will present a noticeable decline in daily impact to the people of the island, but the American military presence would still be more than 20,000 American remaining if you count all the base personnel and dependents associated with a force of approximately 10,000 troops. Concurrently, the United States military has shifted the local community impact of daily military operations from Okinawa and is now impacting the daily lives of the Hawaiian, Guam and Iwakuni populace that undoubtedly will negatively enhance the impact on the daily lives of the people of those localities.

There are four major issues associated with the force laydown that inherently present significant challenges in fulfilling the 2006 Roadmap. Firstly, as previously mentioned, the head of the snake is significantly distanced from the rest of the force directly impacting Command and Control over III MEF forces. The potential remains for Marines and Sailors aboard Okinawa to be involved in activities detrimental to the United States' image. We have seen instances, while extremely rare, of citizens of Okinawa being the victim of crime committed against them by U.S. forces. In 1995, the gang rape of a twelve-year old Okinawa girl by three U.S. Servicemen and the alleged rape of a fourteen year-old girl by a Marine Staff Sergeant fueled intense outrage by the Japanese people and has been rallying cry for the removal of all U.S. forces on Okinawa.[22] What has previously calmed anger over previous crimes has been the sound leadership of Marine Corps General Officers in working through the present issue with local Japanese civil leaders on Okinawa. The Marine Corps is creating a potential situation for unjust criticism based on the perceived or substantiated lack of supervision due to the headquarters elements residing 1,400 miles away from their commands. Each subordinate command will most certainly have commanders and high level officers present for accurate oversight, administration and execution of training and operational responsibilities. Unfortunately, this entire relocation of American forces from Okinawa has been a political game from the very beginning and any instances that cast a dark shadow on the current agreed arrangement of forces will most definitely be used as a political football to suit a particular agenda. By no means should our Marine Corps forces have their headquarters elements separated from the main subordinate units that fall under their command. This arrangement ultimately creates a Command and Control issue that negatively impacts our nation's national security interests and ill-postures our Marine and Navy forces to execute the current Theatre Support Cooperation (TSC) missions our nation is presently engaged, creates a logistical and financial burden on routine administrative and operational force movements throughout the PACOM Area of Operations, and directly impacts the pre-deployment training readiness and capabilities of units assigned within PACOM for deployments to Iraq, Afghanistan and other locales in the fight on terrorism. The issues of proposed recommendations for force laydown, logistical ramifications and training will be discussed further addressed in detail.

The second issue that presents a potential major obstacle is the "Tyranny of Distance" factor in relocating USMC forces further east to Guam. Travel distances create a significant burden operationally and logistically to carry out current Theater Support Cooperation missions (TSC), Bi-lateral training partnerships and operations conducted in the PACOM Area of Operations that are currently minimized by the close proximity of US forces already assigned on Okinawa. Figure 3[23] With the relocation to Guam, a 1,400 mile separation is created for the Headquarters elements of III MEF and their subordinate units assigned to Okinawa and Iwakuni. The reaction from the General Officer down to the Private should be one of surprise and confusion as to how this arrangement actually benefits the daily operations of III MEF in a positive manner and improves the nation's defense poster in PACOM's Area of Operations. The simple answer is that is does not answer the mail in regards to force laydown and if implemented, according the Roadmap of 2006, will significantly impact our nation's ability to provide for the defense of the

Tyranny of Distance

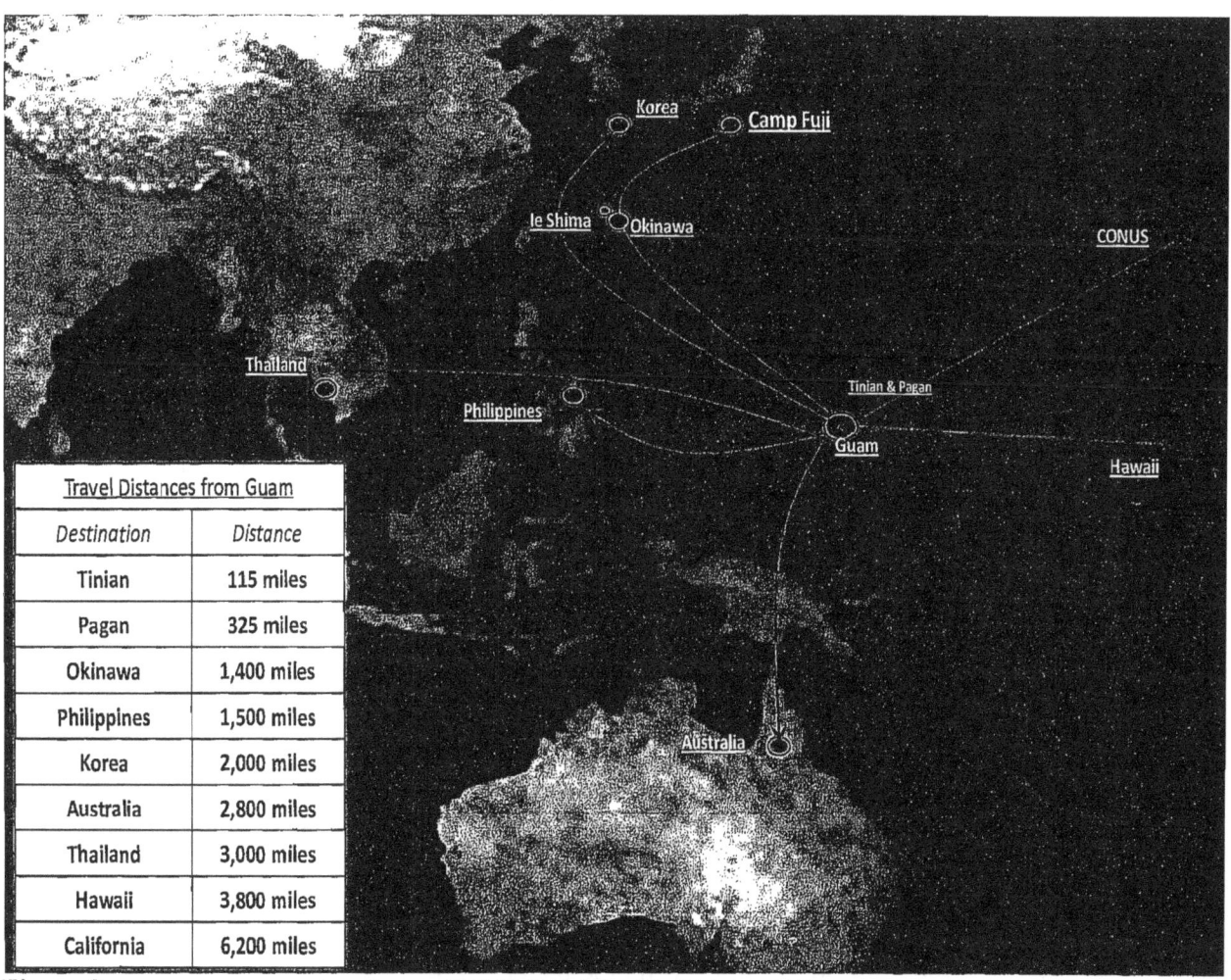

Travel Distances from Guam	
Destination	Distance
Tinian	115 miles
Pagan	325 miles
Okinawa	1,400 miles
Philippines	1,500 miles
Korea	2,000 miles
Australia	2,800 miles
Thailand	3,000 miles
Hawaii	3,800 miles
California	6,200 miles

Figure 3   Source: HQMC/PP&O/Pacific Division 2009

nation in the Pacific region. Increased costs associates with movement of personnel and equipment will hamper an already tight Defense Department budget that has seen wholesale cuts to the Army's Future Combat System (FCS) and the Air Force's F-22 Raptor program and must be considered for future Program Objective Memorandum (POM) budget proposals. Figure 4[24] The U.S. Government, by pursuing the force relocation is unnecessarily increasing the burden on the American taxpayer by needlessly shifting forces throughout the largest COCOM and reducing our forces ability to maximize training hours. The American public should be outraged and should demand of their government the renegotiations with the Government of Japan in regards to the wording of International Agreement that specifically states by name the headquarters elements to be relocated off the island of Okinawa.

Logistically, the move to Guam is going to present major challenges to include increased costs associated in the reuniting of command elements and their subordinates for collective skills training, potential deployments as rejoined units for overseas contingency operations, sometimes referred to as the Global War on Terror (GWOT), and TSC and Bi-lateral exercises involving countries such as Thailand, Australia, Korea, Philippines and a host of other opportunities that greatly enhance our national security interests in the region. New technologies such as the MV-22 Osprey and the Joint High Speed Vessel (JHSV) will greatly enhance our ability move equipment and troops quickly in an intra-theater environment but cannot be relied upon for inter-theatre movement of forces. The traditional means of commercial airlines for the movement of troops along with the use of Navy shipping assets and commercial black-bottom shipping for force reconstitution will be required to make up for the relocation of forces previously assigned to Okinawa. The United States Navy has designated that the JHSV will be used for fast intra-theater transportation of troops, military vehicles and equipment which will counter the opinion

Guam Strategic Lift for Training Cost Summary

(12 month period using current dollar values)

	CNMI	Okinawa	Australia	Thailand	Philippines	Korea	HI	CA
Air Lift	~	8 M	16 M	24 M	8 M	16 M	24 M	40 M
HSV	28 M	~	~	~	~	~	~	~
Movement of Ammo	480 K	~	23 M	17 M	10 M	4 M	~	~
Movement of Equip	~	10 M	21 M	20 M	10 M	12 M	19 M	29 M
Host Nation Support	~	2 M	5 M	2 M	~	2 M	~	~
Other See notes	1,2	~	3	3	3	3	~	~
Total	35 M	20 M	65 M	63 M	28 M	34 M	43 M	69 M

Notes:
1. Range management (O&M, Sustainment, etc) ~ $6M
2. Initial Construction: $1B (not included)
3. Range improvements would be required to meet USMC standards (Exercise Related Construction).

1

Table 1   Source: Headquarters, Marine Forces Pacific 2009

of those that believe the JHSV can be used for movement of forces to Okinawa and reduce the complexity of troop and equipment movements in the theater.[25] According to GlobalSecurity.org's Okinawa fact page, it takes 2 hours to fly to the Korean peninsula from Okinawa, as compared with about 5 hours from Guam, 11 hours from Hawaii, and 16 hours from the continental United States. By shipping, the trip takes approximately 1 1/2 days to make the trip from Okinawa by ship to South Korea, as compared with about 5 days from Guam, 12 days from Hawaii, and 17 days from the continental United States.[26]

Besides increased logistical costs, Theatre lift support requirements will have to be submitted via the existing approval mechanisms that will ultimately be weighed against real-world commitments and prior submitted transportation requests of higher priorities ultimately affecting a unit's ability to move from Guam to Okinawa or other designated areas to marry up with their subordinate units to conduct the assigned mission. The real cost may be the time it takes to deploy the forces required to accomplish a mission that were once stationed at Okinawa, but were removed for convenience in political negotiations between "equal partners" of the United States-Japan alliance.

The fourth and arguably most import issue that confronts the United States Marine Corps in regards to relocation of its forces from Okinawa is its ability to deploy to combat environments having received the full complement of required pre-deployment training. All Marines and Sailors, prior to their deployment into Iraq or Afghanistan, must complete a basic level training program that focuses on individual combat skills up to the unit level collective skills training package. Based upon the specific type of unit and the individual Military Occupational Specialties resident in the unit, training is tailored for that organization's particular mission. For instance, Marine Corps Infantry combat units focus on the Enhanced Marksmanship Program

(EMP), individual, company, battalion and larger combined exercises focusing on the Marine Air Ground Task Force (MAGTF) concept of employment inherent to conducting operations in areas such as Afghanistan and Iraq.

The first critical error of the AIP-directed Roadmap agreement is the previously discussed notion of separating the headquarters elements from the main subordinate elements of III MEF. This violates the basic principle of the Marine Air Ground Task Force concept by separating the crucial lynchpin of oversight, direction and guidance that the Command Element (CE) provides to the other main subordinate elements of the MAGTF. Marine Corps Doctrinal Publication 1 (MCDP-1) states that, *"For operations and training, Marine forces will be formed into Marine air-ground task forces (MAGTFs)...Operating forces should be organized for warfighting and then adapted for peacetime rather than vice versa."[27]* Clearly, what the United States-Japan Roadmap for Realignment Implementation successfully accomplished was the organization of forces in peacetime to be later organized for warfighting as the situation requires. The current administration failed to see the adverse implications of an agreement conceived and jointly signed during the previous administration. The United States has officially and internationally agreed to the splitting up of its nation's 911 Force in Readiness in the largest of the seven Combatant Commands (COCOM) which is home to the rising threats of Islamic Fundamentalist Extremists in the world's largest Islamic region of the world, the continuing threat from North Korea, and the ever-present danger China poses economically and militarily to Taiwan and the United States.

Training capabilities have taken a backseat at the expense of international negotiations. The preponderance of training for the newly relocated Marines is to occur on Guam with the addition of four, small expeditionary ranges aboard the island of Tinian. The Draft Guam Environmental

Impact Study (EIS) addresses individual and limited small unit training aboard Guam and their potential environmental impacts.[28] Areas of training focus include Block I and II predeployment training which include all basic individual warfighting skills concentrating on MOS proficiency and individual skill training which includes driver training, crew served weapons training and other facets of skill sets that a Marine will most likely experience while operating from a Forward Operating Base (FOB).[29] Other training opportunities and ranges focused on Guam are gas chamber facilities, hand grenade range, annual small arms and machine gun qualification ranges, Military Operations in Urban Terrain (MOUT) facility, Demolition Range, and other individual and MOS proficiency enhancing facilities. Guam falls short in providing individual training requirements concerning Anti-Armor live fire and falls short on providing unit level training involving Block I/II live fire predeployment training, fire and movement, combined arms live fire, non-live fire movement due to limited land space and indirect fire training.[30]

On Tinian, there are four planned "expeditionary" training ranges to augment individual skills training occurring on Guam that are a part of the existing Draft Guam EIS study.[31] These four expeditionary ranges fall drastically short to complementing the full training range needs required of Marine Forces on Guam. The argument to providing only limited range capabilities for the Marines on Guam is due to the logic that headquarters elements need fewer training opportunities based on their roles within the Command Element of the MAGTF and that the preponderance of training ranges should be reserved for the subordinated units left behind on Okinawa. This logic is severely flawed based on the requirements for all Marines and Sailors entering combat environments be properly trained in a standardized fashion throughout the Predeployment Training (PTP) continuum.[32] Never mind the fact that every Marine is a Rifleman first and foremost, and must be afforded the opportunities for individual and advanced training expected of every infantryman, whether his or her MOS is Food Service, Military Police, Supply, or a Motor Transport Mechanic. The expectation that Marines from Guam will either forego this essential training of providing essential combat service support in a collective skills, graduating exercise with other combat arms MOS's or embark aboard military or commercial modes of transportation to Okinawa is costly, both in lives and in treasure.

Considering all the limitations of training aboard Guam, the opportunities for bi-lateral training on U.S. soil seems less attractive and severely restricts USMC forces, as well. Figure 4[33] What is needed, and has just recently been added to the November 2009 JGPO Draft EIS, is the recognition that Guam does not fully address all Marine Corps training requirements. This addition did not occur without much internal Pentagon debate, according to USMC officials, particularly championed by Headquarters, Marine Corps requiring that any forces relocating to Guam must have the requisite training capabilities in the region to provide appropriate sustainment and predeployment training. Currently, Headquarters, Marine Corps' Pacific Division (PPO/PD) within Plans, Policies and Operations (PP&O) along with HQMC/Installations and Logistics (HQMC/I&L) and JGPO, based on recent additional EIS funding, are aggressively studying the land space use feasibility for joint training within the CNMI region. The concept studied by PPO/PD with support from I&L and separate from any considerations by the JGPO, is a series of ranges throughout the CNMI with each island possessing the capability for a specific type of training facility with the islands of Pagan and Tinian being the centerpiece.[34] Pagan would facilitate the capstone exercise with the ability to provide for MAGTF-level combined arms, amphibious assault, and inert-live ordnance training packages. Tinian would house maneuver and tactical operations exercises up to battalion size

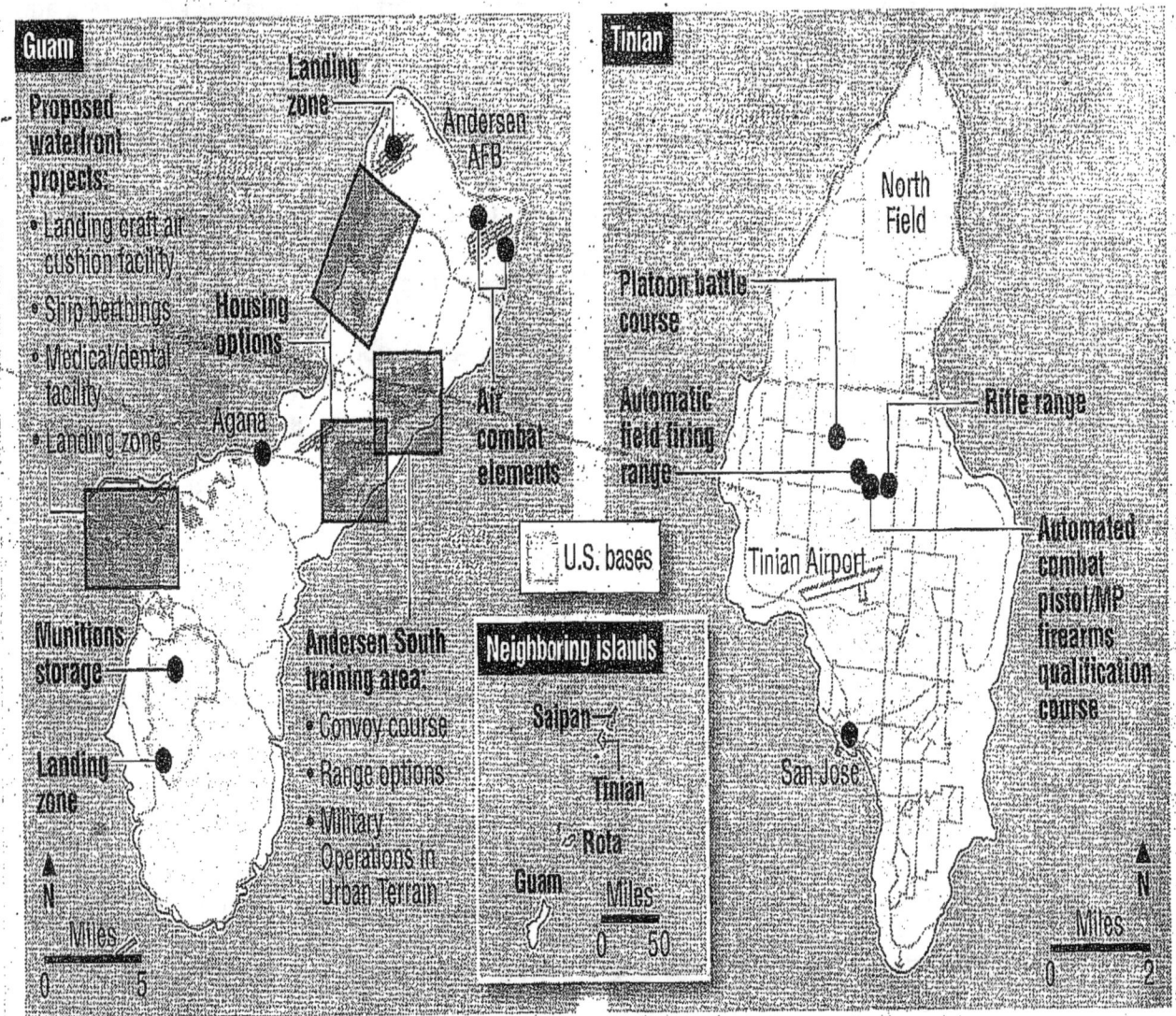

MOVING TO GUAM

The Navy's plan to relocate 17,000 Marines and family members from Okinawa to Guam includes construction of the following housing, training and port infrastructure:

Guam

Proposed waterfront projects:
- Landing craft air cushion facility
- Ship berthings
- Medical/dental facility
- Landing zone

Landing zone

Andersen AFB

Housing options

Agana

Air combat elements

Munitions storage

Landing zone

Andersen South training area:
- Convoy course
- Range options
- Military Operations in Urban Terrain

U.S. bases

Neighboring islands

Saipan

Tinian

Rota

Guam

Miles
0   50

Tinian

North Field

Platoon battle course

Automatic field firing range

Rifle range

Tinian Airport

Automated combat pistol/MP firearms qualification course

San Jose

N

Miles
0   5

N

Miles
0   2

Figure 4   Source: Gidget Fuentes, Marine Corps Times, 2009

units to include mechanized operations and artillery training. Other islands essential to the

supplementing of training aboard Guam would include Saipan for aviation landing practice,

Aguijan for artillery live fire and Farallon De Medinilla (FDM) for use of aviation inert and live

ordnance training.[35] While this approach appears to be an ideal solution and indeed could satisfy

MAGTF training requirements, the fact that as of January 2010, the EIS study is far from complete and approval of this concept and all planning for CNMI course of action is conceptual in design with the assumptions of feasibility all but assumed. At the end of the day, if the CNMI region is not found suitable for training, the Department of Defense will be looking at having to execute an agreement that ill-postures American Forces in the Pacific with inadequate training opportunities aboard its premier Central Pacific base with no alternative but to transport personnel and equipment back to Okinawa to conduct operations and training. Unfortunately, the political wheel is spinning faster than the logistical estimates of supportability can be produced to ensure the Department of Defense is not going down the politically charged Road to Abilene.[36]

A potential course of actions exists that is not actively being considered involves force redistribution including the possibilities to reclaim previously owned bases in the Pacific, for instance Subic Bay Naval Base and Clark Air Force Base in the Republic of the Philippines which the Department of Defense returned in 1993 for use in today's Global War on Terror (GWOT). According to Major Michael F. Kimlick in his 1990 Masters Thesis while attending Marine Corps Command and Staff College, explained, "For the U.S. to remain a Pacific influence through the projection of its air and naval power and to be able to respond to a low-intensity conflict, our military basing, access and transit rights in the Philippines is the key to U.S. power projection capabilities." The potential return to use of the Philippine facilities would take on a gradual approach over a period time to allow for stability within the country through the use of bilateral counterterrorism operations and training, followed by the establishment of the initial facilities utilized as Unit Deployment Program (UDP) opportunities conducted on Okinawa, with the eventual creation of a permanent American base suitable for accompanied tours by service members and their families. The use of facilities and land for potential U.S. military bases that would create pockets of Marine Air Ground Task Force capabilities throughout the Pacific Region in countries such as Australia, Thailand, or South Korea has been previously rejected by the host governments, yet would present ideal conditions for forward American presence. These opportunities should be reconsidered by all governments that would no doubt further enhance our countries relations, assist in providing regional stability, and would ultimately benefit the local economies through employment and business opportunities created by host nation basing.

The current International Agreement was created as a result of pressure by the Japanese Government to quiet a segment of Okinawan society that was displeased with the American presence. Those dissenters failed to see the larger picture in regards to regional security and took advantage of an influential government that further pressed the distracted American government whose attention was focused on a two-front war instead of insisting that the Japanese government rethink their ill-advised need for the removal of American forces from Okinawa. The Obama Administration is currently pressed to deal with a partner government that insists upon writing a check and calling it a day in regards to their roles as an equal partner in regional security issues, limited force participation in fighting terrorism, and the inability to internally settle their concerns in relating to the FRF while putting the U.S. in a holding pattern that is costly in budget planning and facility preparation for the relocation. The entire Roadmap for Realignment must be scrapped and renewal of negotiations for a realignment agreement that puts common sense approaches to defense posture in the Pacific.

NOTES

[1] Hongo, Jun. *Guam move depends on Futenma:Gates*: The Japan Times Online, Thursday 22 October 2009. Quoted U.S. Secretary of Defenses Robert Gates (October 21, 2009), http://search.japantimes.co.jp/cgi-bin/nn20091022a3.html (accessed January 10, 2010).

[2] Headquarters, Marine Corps, Plans, Policies and Operations, Pacific Division. *Defense Policy Review Initiative Orientation Brief.* Washington, D.C.: Department of Defense, 2 Sep 09.

[3] The Special Action Committee on Okinawa (SACO) Final Report December 2, 1996, by Minister of Foreign Affairs Ikeda, Minister of State for Defense Kyuma, Secretary of Defense Perry, and Ambassador Mondale. Tokyo, Japan: Security Consultative Committee (SCC),1996.

[4] The SACO Final Report, 2 Dec 1996

[5] The SACO Final Report, 2 Dec 1996

[6] Earthjustice.org, March 2, 2005, http://www.earthjustice.org/news/press/005/judge_rules_us_defense_department_must_consider_fate_of_okinawan_dugong.html (accessed January 9.2010).

[7] Ministry of Foreign Affairs of Japan, The Japan-U.S. Security Arrangements (including legislation related to the Guidelines for Japan-U.S. Defense Cooperation), http://www.mofa.go.jp/region/n-america/us/security/arrange.html (including legislation related to the Guidelines for Japan-U.S. Defense Cooperation), 2006 (accessed January 9, 2010).

[8] U.S. Department of State, Office of the Spokesman. *United States-Japan Roadmap for Realingment Implementation 2006/437.* Washington, D.C.: Department of State, 2006

[9] *United States-Japan Roadmap for Realignment Implementation 2006/437,*2006

[10] U.S. Department of State. *Agreement Between the Government of the United States of America and the Government of Japan Concerning the Implementation of the Relocation of III Marine Expeditionary Force Personnel and their Dependents from Okinawa to Guam*, February 17, 2009, http://www.state.gov/documents/organization/130450.pdf.

[11] Bruce Klingner, "U.S. Should Stay Firm on Implementation of Okinawa Force Realignment" *Backgrounder*, No. 2352 (December 2009), http://www.heritage.org/Research/AsiaandthePacific/bg2352.cfm.

[12] Prime Minister of Japan and his Cabinet, Joint Press Conference by Prime Minister Yukio Hatoyama of Japan President Barack Obama of the United States of America, http://www.kantei.go.jp/foreign/hatoyama/statement/200911/13usa_kaiken_e.html (accessed January 10, 2010)

[13] Michael Auslin, "The U.S.-Japan Alliance, Relic of a Bygone Era?" *American Enterprise Institute Outlook Series,(January 2010)* http://www.aei.org/outlook/100929 (accessed January 22, 2010).

[14] Bruce Klingner, "Japanese Election Poses Challenges for U.S. Alliance" *Web Memo*, No. 2600 (August 2009). http://www.heritage.org/Research/AsiaandthePacific/wm2600.cfm (accessed January 11, 2010).

[15] Web Memo, No. 2600.

[16] Klingner, December 2009.

[17] Bruce Klingner, "Japan's Security Policy: Navigating the Troubled Waters Ahead" *Backgrounder, No. 2340(November 2009), http://www.heritage.org/Research/AsiaandthePacific/bg2340.cfm.*

[18] Japan Times, "Pentagon Prods Japan on Futenma Deadline", JapanTimes.Co.Jp, January 8, 2010, http://search.japantimes.co.jp/mail/nn20100108a6.html (accessed January 23, 2010)

[19] Eric Talmadge, "Dispute Over Marine Base Sours U.S. Ties With Japan," ChigacoTribune.com, January 6, 2010, http://www.chicagotribune.com/news/chi-tc-nw-japan-marines-0105jan06,0,5613204.story (accessed January 12, 2010).

[20] Major Michael Cho USMC, email message to author, December 4, 2009.

[21] U.S. Government Accountability Office. *Defense Infrastructure: Guam Needs Timely Information from DOD to Meet Challenges in Planning and Financing Off-Base Projects and Programs to Support a Larger Military Presence* (Washington, D.C.: Government Accountability Office, 2009), 1.

[22] Akiko Yamamoto, "Rice, on Japan Visit, Offers U.S. Regrets Over Alleged Rape" WashingtonPost.com, February 28, 2008,http://www.washingtonpost.com/wp-dyn/content/article/2008/02/27/AR2008022702213.html (accessed January 22, 2010).

[23] Headquarters, Marine Corps, Plans, Policies and Operations, Pacific Division, 2 Feb 2009.

[24] Marine Forces Pacific, Strategic Lift Costs Estimate, April 15, 2009.

[25] Navy.mil, Fact File, http://www.navy.mil/navydata/fact_display.asp?cid=4200&tid=1400&ct=4 (accessed January 9, 2010).

[26] GlobalSecuriy.org, Military, http://www.globalsecurity.org/military/facility/okinawa.htm (accessed January 15, 2010).

[27] Headquarters U.S. Marine Corps, *Warfighting,* MCDP1 (Washington, DC: U.S. Marine Corps, June 20, 1997), 55.

[28] Headquarters, Marine Corps, Plans, Policies and Operations, Pacific Division, 2 Feb 2009.

[29] Commandant of the Marine Corps, *The Pre-Deployment Toolkit,* MARADMIN 740/07, December 18, 2007, http://www.marines.mil/news/messages/Pages/2007/MARADMINS85.aspx. (Accessed January 10, 2007)

[30] Headquarters, Marine Corps, *Marine Corps Pacific Posture Strategic Communications Package Draft-Sep 4 2009* (Washington, D.C.: Headquarters, Marine Corps, 2009),37-38

[31] *Marine Corps Pacific Posture Strategic Communications Package Draft-Sep 4 2009,*37.

[32] MARADMIN 740/07

[33] Gidget Fuentes, "Navy outlines plans for base in Guam," *Marine Corps Times,* December 14, 2009.

[34] Defense Policy Review Initiative Orientation Brief 2 Sep 09

[35] *Marine Corps Pacific Posture Strategic Communications Package Draft-Sep 4 2009,*37.

[36] Boise State University, Groupthink, *http://www.boisestate.edu/bsuaop/The%20road%20to%20abilene.pdf* (accessed January 23, 2009)

Bibliography

Auslin, Michael. "The U.S.-Japan Alliance, Relic of a Bygone Era?" *American Enterprise Institute Outlook Series (January 2010):* http://www.aei.org/outlook/100929 (accessed January 22, 2010).

Commandant of the Marine Corps, *The Pre-Deployment Toolkit.* MARADMIN 740/07, December 18, 2007. http://www.marines.mil/news/messages/Pages/2007/MARADMINS85. aspx. (Accessed January 10, 2007)

Fuentes, Gidget. "Navy outlines plans for base in Guam," *Marine Corps Times,* December 14, 2009.

Headquarters, Marine Corps, Plans, Policies and Operations, Pacific Division. *Defense Policy Review Initiative Orientation Brief.* Washington, D.C.: Department of Defense, 2009.

Headquarters U.S. Marine Corps. *Warfighting.* MCDP1. Washington, DC: Headquarters U.S. Marine Corps, June 20, 1997.

Headquarters, Marine Corps. *Marine Corps Pacific Posture Strategic Communications Package Draft-Sep 4 2009.* Washington, D.C.: Headquarters, Marine Corps, 2009.

Hongo, Jun. *Guam move depends on Futenma:Gates*: The Japan Times Online, Thursday 22 October 2009. http://search.japantimes.co.jp/cgi-bin/nn20091022a3.html (accessed January 10, 2010).

Japan Times. "Pentagon Prods Japan on Futenma Deadline." *Japan Times, (*January 2010). http://search.japantimes.co.jp/mail/nn20100108a6.html (accessed January 23, 2010).

Klingner, Bruce. "Japanese Election Poses Challenges for U.S. Alliance" *Web Memo*, No. 2600 (August 2009). http://www.heritage.org/Research/AsiaandthePacific/wm2600.cfm (accessed January 11, 2010).

Klingner, Bruce. "U.S. Should Stay Firm on Implementation of Okinawa Force Realignment" *Backgrounder* No. 2352 (December 2009), http://www.heritage.org/Research/Asiaand thePacific/bg2352.cfm.

Klingner, Bruce. "Japan's Security Policy: Navigating the Troubled Waters Ahead" *Backgrounder, No. 2340 (November 2009): http://www.heritage.org/Research/ AsiaandthePacific/bg2340.cfm.(accessed January 11, 2010)*

Ministry of Foreign Affairs of Japan. The Japan-U.S. Security Arrangements (including legislation related to the Guidelines for Japan-U.S. Defense Cooperation), http://www.mofa.go.jp/region/n-america/us/security/arrange.html (including legislation related to the Guidelines for Japan -U.S. Defense Cooperation). 2006 (accessed January 9, 2010).

Prime Minister of Japan and his Cabinet. *Joint Press Conference by Prime Minister Yukio Hatoyama of Japan President Barack Obama of the United States of America.* Tokyo, Japan: Prime Minister of Japan and his Cabinet, 2009. http://www.kantei.go.jp/foreign/hatoyama/statement/200911/13usa_kaiken_e.html (accessed January 10, 2010)

Talmadge, Eric. "Dispute Over Marine Base Sours U.S. Ties With Japan." *ChigacoTribune.com* (January 2010). http://www.chicagotribune.com/news/chi-tc-nw-japan-marines-0105jan06,0,5613204.story (accessed January 12, 2010).

The Special Action Committee on Okinawa (SACO) Final Report December 2, 1996, by Minister of Foreign Affairs Ikeda, Minister of State for Defense Kyuma, Secretary of Defense Perry, and Ambassador Mondale. Tokyo, Japan: Security Consultative Committee (SCC), 1996.

U.S. Department of State, Office of the Spokesman. *United States-Japan Roadmap for Realignment Implementation 2006/437.* Washington, D.C.: Department of State, 2006

U.S. Department of State. *Agreement Between the Government of the United States of America and the Government of Japan Concerning the Implementation of the Relocation of III Marine Expeditionary Force Personnel and their Dependents from Okinawa to Guam,* http://www.state.gov/documents/organization/130450.pdf, Washington, D.C.: Department of State, 2009.

U.S. Government Accountability Office. *Defense Infrastructure: Guam Needs Timely Information from DOD to Meet Challenges in Planning and Financing Off-Base Projects and Programs to Support a Larger Military Presence.* Washington, D.C.: Government Accountability Office, 2009.

Yamamoto, Akiko. "Rice, on Japan Visit, Offers U.S. Regrets Over Alleged Rape" WashingtonPost.com, February 28, 2008. http://www.washingtonpost.com/wp-dyn/content/article/2008/02/27/AR2008022702213.html (accessed January 22, 2010).